Emanuele Aldrovandi

SORRY WE DIDN'T DIE AT SEA

Translated by Marco Young

Salamander Street

PLAYS

Wordville

Sorry We Didn't Die at Sea was written by Emanuele Aldrovandi in 2015 with the Italian title "Scusate se non siamo morti in mare". The play was a finalist for 2015 Riccione Award and a finalist for 2015 Scenario Award, and was first presented as a staged reading at the 2015 "PIIGS Festival" in Catalan (translated by Carles Fernandez Giua and directed by Rocio Manzano). It was subsequently published in Catalan language anthology "Dramaturgia sobre la crisi" (Dramaturgy of Crisis).

In 2016, the play received its world premiere at Teatro della Cooperativa in Milan, directed by Pablo Solari, starring Matthieu Pastore, Marcello Mocchi, Daniele Pitari, Luz Beatriz Lattanzi, produced by Arte Combustibile and MaMiMò, and was first published in Italian by CUE Press, featuring an introduction by Davide Carnevali. This production toured numerous Italian venues for three consecutive seasons until 2019.

In 2018, the play was presented in French (in collaboration with MAV Maison Antoine Vitez) at "La mousson d'été festival" in Pont-a-Mousson, directed by Ivica Buljan, starring Charlie Nelson, Alain Fromager, Didier Manuel and Johanna Nizard.

In 2021, the play was produced in German (translated by Sabine Heymann) at Theater für Niedersachsen, Hildesheim, directed by Hüseyin Michael Cirpici and Anna Siegrot, starring Linda Riebau, Martin Schwartengräber, Haytham Hmeidan and Jeremias Beckford.

In 2022, the English translation (by Marco Young) premiered at Seven Dials Playhouse in London from 12-16 July 2023, directed by Daniel Emery, produced by Saskia Baylis, starring Will Bishop, Yasmine Haller, Felix Garcia Guyer and Marco Young with lighting design by Mary Bennet and sound design by Jamie Lu. It went on to have its first full production at Park Theatre, produced by The Playwright's Laboratory and Riva Theatre, opening on 13th September 2023. The cast and creative team was:

The Tall One | **Will Bishop**
The Burly One | **Felix Garcia Guyer**
The Beautiful One | **Yasmine Haller**
The Stocky One | **Marco Young**

Writer | **Emanuele Aldrovandi**
Translator | **Marco Young**
Director | **Daniel Emery**
Producer | **Katharine Farmer**
Set And Costume Designer | **Alys Whitehead**
Sound Designer And Creative Associate |**Jamie Lu**
Lighting Designer | **Catja Hamilton**
Production Manager | **Ian Taylor and Lewis Champney for eStage**
Stage Manager | **Nell Thomas**
Marketing Manager | **Liam McLaughlin**
Photography | **Lidia Crisafulli**

CAST

Will Bishop | Actor *(The Tall One)*

Will Bishop is a London-based actor represented by Global Artists. Recent credits include: *Rani Takes On The World* (Big Finish Audio), *Just Be Good* (Hen & Chickens Theatre) as well as playing The Tall One in the initial run of *Sorry We Didn't Die at Sea* (Seven Dials Playhouse). He is also a writer, and alongside his writing partner Colm Gleeson has penned the plays *I Have Heard You Calling in the Night* (Union Theatre) and *Anadiplosis* (Hen & Chickens Theatre). He has also written two short films, and is currently developing projects for television and radio.

Felix Garcia Guyer | Actor *(The Burly One)*

Felix is a British-Chilean actor who trained at Bristol Old Vic Theatre School graduating in 2018. He orginated the role of The Burly One at the Seven Dials Playhouse run of *Sorry We Didn't Die at Sea*. Credits incude: *The Spanish Princess* (STARZ), *Sanctuary* (Studio Canal), *The Man Who Fell to Earth* (Paramount+), *LIFT* (Netflix), *Treasure Island* (Miracle Theatre), *Kraven the Hunter* (Sony Marvel), *DI RAY* (ITV) and *Homegrown* (BFI short film). He is also a combat choreographer and fight performer and has choreographed for both stage and screen.

Yasmine Haller | Actor *(The Beautiful One)*

Yasmine Haller is a Swiss and Egyptian actor. She first started her training in Paris at Cours Florent, then moved to London to pursue the MFA in Professional Acting at LAMDA, from which she graduated in 2020. That same year, she was shortlisted for the Spotlight Prize, alongside finalists from the top UK drama schools. Recent acting credits include the short film *A Mistake with the Chairs* directed by Alistair Petrie, *This Last Piece of Sky* performed at The Space, the initial run of *Sorry We Didn't Die at Sea* at Seven Dials Playhouse, and *All Will Be Well* created by NOMAD, the theatre company she co-founded.

In September 2022, she integrated the renowned Comédie-Franзaise in Paris for a yearlong contract, working alongside directors Éric Ruf, Clément Hervieu-Léger, Simon Delétang, Christophe Honoré and Lisaboa Houbrechts. She recently performed and sang in the cabaret show *La Ballade de Souchon*, about French singer Alain Souchon, directed by Françoise Gillard.

Marco Young | Actor *(The Stocky One)*

Marco trained at Bristol Old Vic Theatre School. Stage credits include: *Sorry We Didn't Die at Sea* (Seven Dials Playhouse), *Another America* (Park Theatre), *The Life and Adventures of Santa Claus* (Pitlochry Festival Theatre), *My Cousin Rachel* (Bath Theatre Royal & UK Tour), *The Stranger on the Bridge* (Salisbury Playhouse/Tobacco Factory & SW Tour), *Macbeth, Romeo and Juliet* (both Guildford Shakespeare Company), *A Girl, Standing,* (Theatre503), *Me & My Left Ball* (Tristan Bates), *Measure for Measure, Henry V* (both Cambridge Arts Theatre). TV includes: *Big Boys* S2 (Channel 4/Roughcut). Video Game: *Company of Heroes 3* (Relic Entertainment). Workshops: *Lasagne* (King's Head), *HighTide Rising* (HighTide Theatre).

CREATIVE TEAM

Emanuele Aldrovandi | Writer

Emanuele Aldrovandi is an Italian playwright. He is Artistic Director of Associazione Teatrale Autori Vivi. In 2013, with *Homicide House*, he won the Riccione/Tondelli Award. He has also won the Pirandello National Award with *Felicità*, the Fersen Award with *Il Generale*, the Hystrio Award and the Mario Fratti Award with *Farfalle*. He has written original plays and adaptations for leading Italian theatres such as ERT Emilia Romagna National Theater, Elfo Puccini Theatre and Teatro Stabile di Torino National Theater. He has collaborated with established Italian theatre companies like MaMiMт and ATIR, and translated plays including *Trainspotting, The Curious Incident of the Dog in the Night-Time* and *The Laramie Project* into Italian. He was one of the European playwrights selected by Fabulamundi Playwriting Europe, and his plays have been translated, performed and published in English, German, French, Spanish, Polish, Slovenian, Czech, Catalan and Arabic.

Marco Young | Translator

Marco is a British-Italian translator and actor. He has been translating commercially since 2018. He began translating Italian theatre into English in early 2020, and is particularly interested in politically engaged contemporary Italian pieces discussing migration, journeys and the threat of the far-right. He was a mentee on the 2022-23 Foreign Affairs Theatre Translator Mentorship Programme, for which his translation of *Suburban Miracles* by Gabriele Di Luca was showcased at Camden People's Theatre in January 2023. His translation of *Allarmi* by Emanuele Aldrovandi received a rehearsed reading at Omnibus Theatre in July 2023. This translation of *Sorry We Didn't Die at Sea*, the piece's first British-English version, was first staged at Seven Dials Playhouse in July 2022. He was a member of Mercury Theatre Colchester's Producer Development Programme 2022-2023.

Daniel Emery | Director

Daniel is a European director and translator from South London. He is Associate Director of both Peckham Levels Theatre and Shipwright, Deptford, staging radical live work in South East London. Daniel is a committee member of translation collective Art Translated. He is co-director, with Marco Young, of Riva Theatre, a production company focussed on bringing plays from abroad to UK stages. He holds an MSc in Political Sociology, with a research focus on necropolitics and the sociological valency of artistic production. Daniel's practice spans theatre and comedy. As director, his work includes: *Pillow Talk* (Pleasance, Edinburgh; Second City, Chicago; UCB, New York), *Allarmi* (Omnibus Theatre), *Peter Pan: A Cabaret Pantomime* (Shipwright), *John Tothill: The Last Living Libertine* (Pleasance), and the initial run of *Sorry We Didn't Die at Sea* (Seven Dials Playhouse).

Katharine Farmer | Producer

Katharine Farmer is the Artistic Director of The Playwright's Laboratory, a company that provides a network for global theatre professionals who support, develop and programme new work. Through TPL Katharine has developed and produced readings and workshops of 25 new plays in the UK, and works in partnership with over 30 world-class theatres including Hampstead Theatre and Papatango New Writing Prize. Katharine also directs and produces full-scale productions under her theatre company Blue Touch Paper Productions. Most recently, Katharine's production of *Never Not Once* at Park Theatre received 4 and 5 star reviews from national press such as The Guardian. Previous directing credits include Southwark Playhouse, The Other Palace, Warwick Arts Centre and The Theatre Chipping Norton. Katharine is currently an Artistic Associate at Arcola Theatre.

A NOTE FROM THE TRANSLATOR

I first read *Scusate Se Non Siamo Morti in Mare* in November 2021. Two days later, the highest number of deaths from a single incident in the English Channel was recorded; a dinghy had sunk between France and the UK, killing 27 migrants. That whole month, the news was littered with similarly tragic incidents. I realised that this piece, in its portrayal of a precarious maritime journey, was just as relevant to the British social conscience as it was to the Italian. In both countries, recent years have seen the sea turned into a contested political site, above and beyond the promotion of empathy and humanitarian concerns.

This piece has therefore only gained in resonance since its writing at the height of the Mediterranean migrant crisis in 2015. Here in the UK, we are continuing to see the refracted image of that ongoing crisis on our shores. I felt it was important to produce an English version of this play so that the conversations it invites, specifically around the contingency of migrant status and the fragility of societal stability, could be introduced into that context.

Yet in doing so, I found that its power is that it is not a straightforwardly 'political' piece. Yes, it hints at some sort of economic collapse that has inverted the direction of migration, encouraging a politicised reflection on states' attitudes to the individuals undergoing such journeys. But it is also a far broader philosophical reflection about survival, about how violence could erupt at any moment given the 'right' circumstances, and about the sublime power of the natural world. It's deeply dark in its comedy and epic in the brutality at the play's end.

Or more accurately, it's all these things at once, and none of them. We never really know where we stand: Aldrovandi draws us into interactions between characters that feel simultaneously real yet archetypal, and then lifts us into abstraction with the tone of a geography class, or a macabre nature documentary, led by this deeply unsettling, clown-like figure of the people smuggler.

The result is a text which I believe spans multiple genres, none of them ever feeling under-delivered. In translation, it has been an exciting challenge to illuminate those different registers and make them accessible to an English audience, whilst ensuring that they lose none of the nuance of the original Italian. I've relished the opportunity to do so, and to introduce this powerful piece by one of Italy's foremost writers to the UK.

Marco Young
2023

ABOUT PARK THEATRE

Park Theatre was founded by Artistic Director, Jez Bond and Creative Director Emeritus, Melli Marie. The building opened in May 2013 and, with 12 West End transfers, two National Theatre transfers and 14 national tours in ten years, quickly garnered a reputation as a key player in the London theatrical scene. Park Theatre has received six Olivier nominations, won numerous Off West End Offie Awards, and won The Stage's Fringe Theatre of the Year and Accessible Theatre Award.

Park Theatre is an inviting and accessible venue, delivering work of exceptional calibre in the heart of Finsbury Park. We work with writers, directors and designers of the highest quality to present compelling, exciting and beautifully told stories across our two intimate spaces.

Our programme encompasses a broad range of work from classics to revivals with a healthy dose of new writing, producing in-house as well as working in partnership with emerging and established producers. We strive to play our part within the UK's theatre ecology by offering mentoring, support and opportunities to artists and producers within a professional theatre-making environment.

Our Creative Learning strategy seeks to widen the number and range of people who participate in theatre, and provides opportunities for those with little or no prior contact with the arts.

In everything we do we aim to be warm and inclusive; a safe, welcoming and wonderful space in which to work, create and visit.

★★★★★ "A five-star neighbourhood theatre." The Independent

As a registered charity [number 1137223] with no regular public subsidy, we rely on the kind support of our donors and volunteers. To find out how you can get involved visit parktheatre.co.uk

FOR PARK THEATRE

Artistic Director Jez Bond
Executive Director Catherine McKinney

Creative Learning

Community Engagement Manager Carys Rose Thomas
Creative Learning Leaders Amy Allen, Kieran Rose, Vanessa Sampson

Development

Development Director Tania Dunn
Development & Producing Coordinator Ellen Harris

Finance

Finance Director Elaine Lavelle
Finance Officer Nicola Brown

General Management

General Manager Tom Bailey
Deputy General Manager David Hunter
Producer Programmer Amelia Cherry
Administrator Mariah Sayer
Access Coordinator David Deacon
Duty Venue Managers Daisy Bates, Leiran Gibson, Gareth Hackney, Zara Naeem, Laura Riseborough, Natasha Green, David Hunter, Shaun Joynson, Leena Makoff, Wayne Morris, Nick Raistrick

Park Pizza

Supervisors George Gehm, Daisy Bates
Park Pizza & Bar Team Ewan Brand, John Burman, Francesca Fratichenti, Anna Goodman, Alex Kristoffy, Isabella Meyersohn, Maddie Stoneman, Sophie Sullivan

Sales & Marketing

Sales & Marketing Director Dawn James
Interim Sales & Marketing Director (Maternity Cover) Sammie Squire

With thanks to all of our supporters, donors and volunteers.

Sorry We Didn't Die at Sea

Emanuele Aldrovandi

translated by Marco Young

CHARACTERS

The Tall One

The Burly One

The Beautiful One

The Stocky One

ACT ONE – AT THE PORT

SCENE ONE

THE TALL ONE, THE BEAUTIFUL ONE and THE STOCKY ONE. THE TALL ONE has a wheeled suitcase, THE BEAUTIFUL ONE has a bag and THE STOCKY ONE isn't carrying anything. They are facing THE BURLY ONE.

THE BURLY ONE: So it's a thousand dollars now, and a thousand when we get there. No euros. They're worthless. The first thousand is a deposit, so I know you're not going to screw me over. And for compensation in case you die. I'll collect the second thousand on arrival to show I'm not screwing you over either. Because I could if I wanted to; I'd just have to kill you and keep all your stuff. I'd even save some money. But then word would get around and I'd be out of a job, wouldn't I? That's the only reason you can trust me: you're worth more to me alive than dead. (*takes money from THE TALL ONE*) Ooh, fresh from the cash machine, I won't even bother counting this. (*takes money from THE BEAUTIFUL ONE, and then from THE STOCKY ONE, who offers a bag of coins*) What the hell is this?

THE STOCKY ONE: A thousand dollars.

THE BURLY ONE: In small change?

THE STOCKY ONE: Only the last hundred is in change.

THE BURLY ONE: Do I look like I've got time to count all this?

THE STOCKY ONE: Count it on the way. That way you won't get bored.

THE BURLY ONE: If there's even a single cent missing, I'll throw you overboard. All of you, empty your pockets and open your bags.

THE TALL ONE: Why?

2

THE BURLY ONE: Because I say so. Otherwise you're not getting in my container.

THE TALL ONE: Well, I'll have my money back then.

THE BURLY ONE: I told you, that was a deposit. (*To THE STOCKY ONE*) Where's your bag?

THE STOCKY ONE: I don't have one.

THE BURLY ONE frisks and searches THE STOCKY ONE to see if he's carrying anything. He finds a knife.

THE BURLY ONE: Well, well. I'll keep this.

THE STOCKY ONE: Fine. I want it back when we get there, though.

THE BEAUTIFUL ONE opens her bag. THE BURLY ONE turns it upside down and the contents spill out. Some clothes, books and a clump of photos held together with a piece of string. THE BURLY ONE frisks THE BEAUTIFUL ONE too and finds a hairbrush in her pocket.

THE BURLY ONE: A hair brush? Worried you won't find one out there?

THE BEAUTIFUL ONE: I wanted to have this one with me.

THE BURLY ONE: (*to THE TALL ONE*) What're you still doing here?

THE TALL ONE: I'm staying.

THE BURLY ONE: Open up, then.

THE TALL ONE: I don't want you touching me, though.

THE TALL ONE opens his suitcase. It contains several shirts, t-shirts, pairs of trousers, suits, and a laptop. THE BURLY ONE studies the contents but doesn't empty it out onto the floor.

THE BURLY ONE: You still don't get it, do you? It doesn't matter what you want. (*He is about to frisk THE TALL ONE, but then stops and decides not to*) We're leaving in ten minutes.

THE BURLY ONE exits. THE BEAUTIFUL ONE starts picking up her belongings and putting them back into her bag. THE TALL ONE moves towards her.

THE TALL ONE: Here, let me help you.

THE BEAUTIFUL ONE: I'm all done, thanks.

THE TALL ONE: You're not European.

THE BEAUTIFUL ONE: No.

THE TALL ONE: Where are you from?

THE BEAUTIFUL ONE: North Africa.

THE TALL ONE: Which country?

THE BEAUTIFUL ONE: Have you ever been to North Africa?

THE TALL ONE: No.

THE BEAUTIFUL ONE: There's no point telling you, then.

THE TALL ONE: Your English is good, though.

THE BEAUTIFUL ONE: I've lived here a long time.

THE TALL ONE: Where do you think he's taking us?

THE BEAUTIFUL ONE: Where do you think?

THE TALL ONE: Somewhere better than here.

THE BEAUTIFUL ONE: Anywhere would be better than here.

THE TALL ONE: Apart from North Africa, otherwise you would've stayed there.

THE BEAUTIFUL ONE: I was very young when I came over. It was my parents' choice.

THE TALL ONE: Do they regret it now?

THE BEAUTIFUL ONE: They're dead.

THE TALL ONE: Oh, I'm so sorry. Do you remember it?

THE BEAUTIFUL ONE: What?

THE TALL ONE: The journey.

THE BEAUTIFUL ONE: I remember leaving. We were on the shore just like now, but there were lots more of us, people from all over Africa, bunched together waiting for a boat which definitely wouldn't fit us all. Europe was like a mirage, some rich place. Without wars. Full of possibility. That feels like centuries ago now.

THE TALL ONE: Well, we were falling apart even then. You just couldn't tell because your countries were already in pieces.

THE BEAUTIFUL ONE: ...Thanks.

THE TALL ONE: Well, hey, now we're in pieces together.

THE BEAUTIFUL ONE: It's cyclical. Africa is on the way up again.

THE TALL ONE: Europe isn't, though.

THE BEAUTIFUL ONE: You've still got time to change your mind.

THE TALL ONE: About what?

THE BEAUTIFUL ONE: You don't have to leave just because you've paid some of the money. Go home.

THE TALL ONE: How do you know I even have a home?

THE BEAUTIFUL ONE: Your life's worth more than a thousand dollars.

THE TALL ONE: Is yours not?

THE BEAUTIFUL ONE: I'm not going to die.

THE TALL ONE: Well, I hope I won't either.

5

THE BEAUTIFUL ONE: I hope you don't too, but these journeys are dangerous.

THE TALL ONE: I know.

THE BEAUTIFUL: If you knew, you wouldn't have folded your shirts like that.

THE TALL ONE: What do you mean?

THE STOCKY ONE: What was he supposed to do? Just cram them all into a bag? They're not rags. They're Egyptian cotton, aren't they?

THE TALL ONE: They are.

THE STOCKY ONE: See? Clocked right away that it was Egyptian cotton. I've got a whole wardrobe of shirts like that. I'd have folded them exactly the same. (*Shivering*) Should've brought a heavier coat, though. To be honest, if I'd had more time, I wouldn't even be here. But things went as they did, no point whining, right? You're lucky he didn't frisk you. I needed that knife. You don't have a knife, do you?

THE TALL ONE: No.

THE STOCKY ONE: Listen, can I be blunt? I need 600 dollars. I gave the guy a thousand – it was actually nine hundred and ninety, but he's not gonna count it – and I pretended I've got another thousand, but I don't. I've only got four hundred.

That's why I needed my knife, but he frisked me. And I could hardly be like 'no, I'm not giving it to you", could I? He'd have got suspicious. No? Hey, look at me: what do you think?

THE TALL ONE: Well, I'm sorry, that's tricky. If you owe him another thousand and you've only got four hundred...

THE STOCKY ONE: But maybe it's better this way. I don't like violence. There's other solutions, right? Maybe someone else could lend me the six hundred I need.

THE TALL ONE: How are you gonna find someone who's got that kind of money?

THE STOCKY ONE: Do you?

THE TALL ONE: No.

THE STOCKY ONE: Come on, you must have a thousand, at least.

THE TALL ONE: Well yes, obviously, but I need it.

THE STOCKY ONE: How much else have you got?

THE TALL ONE: I gave the other thousand to him.

THE STOCKY ONE: But what else have you got?

THE TALL ONE: I don't have any other money.

THE STOCKY ONE: So when we get there you'll be broke? Not a penny to your name?

THE TALL ONE: Yeah, so?

THE STOCKY ONE: Well, how will you manage?

THE TALL ONE: That's my problem.

THE STOCKY ONE: Come on, don't fuck me around. You don't seem like the type of guy who sets off on a two thousand dollar journey with exactly two thousand dollars. You must have at least three thousand – two thousand to give to the big guy and a thousand for when we get there.

THE TALL ONE: That would've been handy.

THE STOCKY ONE: I told you, don't fuck me around. First you apologize and then you fuck me around?

THE TALL ONE: I'm not fucking you around.

THE STOCKY ONE: How about this: you lend me the money now, and when we get there, I'll pay you back double.

THE TALL ONE: Seriously, I only have a thousand left.

THE STOCKY ONE: Do you think I'm an idiot?

THE TALL ONE: No...

THE STOCKY ONE: Yes you do.

THE TALL ONE: Look, if I was that rich, I wouldn't be trying to leave the country, would I?

THE STOCKY ONE: Even if you had two thousand dollars, you still wouldn't be rich. And I reckon you do.

THE TALL ONE: OK, fine, let's say I do – and, again, I don't – if I did, why should I give it to you?

THE STOCKY ONE: That's a very easy question. With a very easy answer.

THE TALL ONE: Go on.

THE STOCKY ONE: Because if you don't, I'll kill you.

Pause.

THE STOCKY ONE: I'm kidding, come on, don't be so tense. If you don't want to help me, fine. But you're the one losing out, I'm telling you now, because if you give me the money now I'll pay you back double. 1200 dollars. Anyway, think about it. We'll talk about it when we've set off.

Silence.

THE TALL ONE turns to THE BEAUTIFUL ONE.

THE TALL ONE: Thanks.

THE BEAUTIFUL ONE: For what?

THE TALL ONE: The advice earlier.

THE BEAUTIFUL ONE: You ignored it.

THE TALL ONE: I still appreciated it.

THE BEAUTIFUL ONE: Well, I didn't say it for the sake of it. I said it because my parents made the biggest mistake of their lives when they left. And I wish someone had asked them if they were sure.

THE TALL ONE: Because you think about what you might gain, not what you leave behind.

THE BURLY ONE enters.

THE BURLY ONE: Right, come on, get in! We're leaving. It's rough seas, so the coastguard'll stay at harbour, they won't bother us. If you need to be sick, can you all please do it in the same corner. Same if you need to piss or shit. But if you need to die, better to do it in that corner. Just a question of dignity, isn't it? And also so you don't get covered in shit before we throw your body overboard. Anyone wanna change their mind?

THE TALL ONE: No.

SCENE TWO

THE BURLY ONE.

THE BURLY ONE: In commercial transactions with overseas
entities, the manner chosen to transport goods is of vital
importance, not only to ensure proper management of the
goods themselves and to ensure they reach their destination
in perfect condition, as agreed, but also from an economic
standpoint. International transportation of goods may take
place by land, sea or air. Usually, transportation by land is
economically preferable for localised transactions; transport
by air is selected for small quantities or highly perishable
substances; while maritime transport becomes the most
convenient choice when negotiating long distances and
large quantities of material. The original concept of the
container can be traced back to the American transportation
entrepreneur, Malcolm McLean. In 1956, sat in a truck
waiting for his goods to be loaded onto a ship, McLean
realised that it would have been much simpler to load the
entire truck onto the ship, rather than individual items,
one by one. The most widely used type of container is the
ISO container, an acronym which stands for International
Organisation for Standardization. The ISO is a rectangular
metal structure, the measurements of which were
standardised internationally in 1967. Compared to the average
measurements of other container types, which tend to be a
length of 8 feet and a height of 8 feet and 6 inches, ISO
containers come in two standard lengths of 20 feet and 40
feet. The use of such containers has reached such importance
in the field of maritime transport that some current estimates
suggest they carry almost ninety percent of worldwide
maritime cargo, amounting to around 2 hundred million
containers a year. (*Turning to the others*) Time to go.

ACT TWO – IN THE CONTAINER

SCENE ONE

THE TALL ONE, THE STOCKY ONE and THE BEAUTIFUL ONE. THE BEAUTIFUL ONE and THE STOCKY ONE are lying down, one on each side of the container. THE TALL ONE is pacing, and looking around the container. He lets out a deep sigh. He doesn't feel well.

THE STOCKY ONE: Are you alright?

THE TALL ONE: How do you think the air gets in?

THE STOCKY ONE: It doesn't.

THE TALL ONE: What do you mean it doesn't?

THE STOCKY ONE: These things are sealed shut, that's the point of them.

THE TALL ONE: Yeah, to carry objects. But this time it's carrying people, so I don't know, maybe he's cut a hole in it somewhere.

THE STOCKY ONE: A container with a hole in it is useless.

THE TALL ONE: Well, how much longer can three of us last in here with no air?

THE STOCKY ONE: Depends how much breath you waste.

THE TALL ONE stops moving and freezes on the spot.

THE STOCKY ONE: Come on, I'm kidding. Relax, there's loads of air. Don't worry.

THE TALL ONE: I'm not worried.

THE STOCKY ONE: You're turning green.

THE TALL ONE: It's just seasickness.

THE STOCKY ONE: You're lucky it's not that rough right now. Imagine what it'll be like in the middle of the ocean.

THE TALL ONE: How do you know? We might follow the coastline.

THE STOCKY ONE: What coastline?

THE TALL ONE: I don't know... head North.

THE STOCKY ONE: And then?

THE TALL ONE: I don't know. Or maybe South. Maybe we'll go round the bottom of Africa and then... well, I don't know, OK? There's tonnes of places over there.

THE STOCKY ONE: Nah, too far. I think much more likely we'll cross the ocean. Are you gonna be sick?

THE TALL ONE: No. I don't think so. I just need to stare at a fixed point, or the horizon or just get some fresh air.

He pauses, breathes in, tries to stay calm.

THE TALL ONE: My head is spinning.

THE STOCKY ONE: Fishermen say the best remedy for seasickness is anchovies in brine.

THE TALL ONE: No thanks, I'm not hungry.

THE STOCKY ONE: And I obviously don't have any anchovies in brine. I've got some crackers, though.

THE TALL ONE: I don't want any.

THE STOCKY ONE: I know you don't want any, but you've got to eat something. Trust me. If you sit down and eat something you'll feel better straight away. Come here.

*THE TALL ONE sits down next to THE STOCKY ONE. THE
STOCKY ONE produces a pack of crackers and offers them to THE TALL
ONE.*

THE TALL ONE: Thanks.

*THE TALL ONE takes a cracker. He holds it up and stares at it. He stares
at it for quite a while, then takes a bite. He swallows the first bite and then
suddenly eats the rest of the packet ravenously, finishing all the crackers.*

THE STOCKY ONE: Is that any better?

THE TALL ONE: Yeah. Yeah, a bit. Thanks.

THE STOCKY ONE: Good. I couldn't believe it earlier, when
you opened your suitcase and you had all those shirts, a
computer... I expected to meet people who had nothing. I
was a bit worried, to be honest, because desperate people
are dangerous, aren't they? But I've been lucky. I mean, if
things had gone differently, I'd be on my own private jet
right now... best not think about it. Gotta be positive. I own a
beachside villa, you know. Two pools. Twenty bedrooms. Full
of sculptures and paintings... do you like paintings?

THE TALL ONE: Yes.

THE STOCKY ONE: Not just as an investment, I mean. From an
artistic perspective.

THE TALL ONE: Yes, I like them.

THE STOCKY ONE: Me too. If I think of all the paintings I
couldn't bring with me, I feel like crying.

THE TALL ONE: What happened?

THE STOCKY ONE: Well, they took my house and now they're
looking for me. That's why I ran away. Nothing but the
clothes on my back, the money in my wallet. They tried to
freeze my European assets. But I'm not an idiot – I'd already
moved my money, hadn't I? Guess where I moved it to?

THE TALL ONE: Where?

THE STOCKY ONE: Where do you think?

THE TALL ONE: I don't know. Where?

THE STOCKY ONE: To the place we're going.

THE BEAUTIFUL ONE: Which is secret.

THE TALL ONE: Weren't you sleeping?

THE BEAUTIFUL ONE: You're talking too loudly.

THE TALL ONE: Sorry.

THE BEAUTIFUL ONE: At least I didn't miss the show.

THE TALL ONE: What show?

THE BEAUTIFUL ONE: All the shit he's making up with to steal six hundred dollars off you. I hope you're not stupid enough to believe him.

THE STOCKY ONE: How do you know it's all shit?

THE BEAUTIFUL ONE: Because I don't like people like you.

THE STOCKY ONE: Prejudices are dangerous, though. If I gave into mine, I'd hate you just because you're a dirty fucking immigrant. People like you invaded and ruined our continent. So what if I don't like you either? What if I proved it? I could come over there and kick your head in. But I won't.

THE BEAUTIFUL ONE is livid. THE TALL ONE is shocked.

THE BEAUTIFUL ONE: What are you talking about?! It wasn't immigrants who ruined/

THE STOCKY ONE: /Everyone's entitled to their point of view.

THE BEAUTIFUL ONE storms away.

THE TALL ONE: She's got nothing to do with it.

14

THE STOCKY ONE: Exactly. That's why I'm leaving her alone. And she should leave me the fuck alone too.

Silence.

THE TALL ONE: How can you have sent money ahead, if our destination is secret?

THE STOCKY ONE: It's secret for you two. Not for me.

THE TALL ONE: And why are they looking for you?

THE STOCKY ONE: I was contracted to one of the failing European companies. I helped them move their capital and reopen overseas under a new name. With the same machinery. Transported it in containers just like this one.

THE TALL ONE: Bankruptcy fraud.

THE STOCKY ONE: Yeah, well, you could call it that. I'd prefer to say that I... enabled a changing of the times.

THE TALL ONE: And you don't think things like that did much more harm than immigrants coming/

THE STOCKY ONE: /Everyone's entitled to their point of view, like I said. But one thing's for sure: if I hadn't done it, someone else would have. And I wouldn't have a driver waiting for me at the port in an Audi A7. Latest model, tinted windows.

THE TALL ONE: And yet you need six hundred dollars.

THE STOCKY ONE: Well, yeah. Imagine that! I own a private jet and I'm forced to beg you for money.

THE TALL ONE: Well, look, even if you swore to pay me back/

THE STOCKY ONE: /Oh no, I won't just pay you back, I'll pay you back double. In fact, you know what? Given the situation double still isn't enough. If you lend me six hundred, I'll pay you back three times over. As soon as we get off the ship, three times over. 1800 dollars. 1800 dollars in return for six hundred. What a deal.

THE TALL ONE: It would be, if I had six hundred.

THE STOCKY ONE: Woah, hold on, come on, we've been talking this whole time, we've become friends, and you're still taking the piss?

THE TALL ONE: I'm not taking the piss.

THE STOCKY ONE: You're fucking taking the piss.

THE BURLY ONE enters.

THE BURLY ONE: Guanciale, pecorino and pepper. And a whole lot of love. The instructions are very simple: heat some oil in a pan, add the guanciale, cut it into two to three centimetre chunks, and fry until it becomes nice and crisp, and the fat melts into the oil. Some people don't use oil, and just use the fat of the guanciale, melted in the pan, with a tablespoon of white wine vinegar to counteract the fatty taste of the guanciale. I personally like it just as it is, without any vinegar. And I use a lot of oil. Next, cook the bucatini in salted water and drain it when al dente, saving one cup of cooking water. Add the pasta into the pan with the guanciale and mix well, adding a generous amount of pecorino, pepper and some of the cooking water to create a nice creamy texture. Voila. Bucatini alla Gricia. Also known as the white Amatriciana. Do you know what the second worst thing about my job is? Loneliness. That's why I've started talking to myself: I learn things off by heart and then repeat them. And as I repeat them I change them. Both because I don't remember them perfectly, but also mainly because I'm influenced by what's going on outside. Whether it's hot or cold, whether I'm hungry. Are you hungry? Do you want another recipe? Or do you want me to run you through the organoleptic properties of wine? Knowing things means I can make connections, become inter-disciplinary. I've learnt so many new words, looking on the internet, on Wikipedia, and I learn the stuff that interests me. Sometimes it's stuff I don't give a fuck about.

But at the end of the day, nothing can beat human contact, can it? Ask me a question. Go on, ask me a question. Please?

THE TALL ONE: How long left?

THE BURLY ONE: Too long to say. Ask more interesting questions.

THE TALL ONE: How many containers do you own?

THE BURLY ONE: One. I'm all yours. But if things go well, in a month's time I'll buy another one. I'll become a little businessman. (*To THE BEAUTIFUL ONE*) Tell me about that hairbrush you had in your pocket. What's its story? You can make it up if you like, as long as it's a good story.

THE BEAUTIFUL ONE: It belonged to my grandmother. She'd use it to comb her hair every night before bed, singing as she combed. I'd take it and use it in secret, because I wanted my hair to become like hers, long and thick as wool, and I thought it was the comb that did it. I was holding it when my mother told me we were going to Europe. I clung onto it that day and I'll keep it forever. It still smells of home. Of my grandmother. She didn't want us to leave. I still remember the day one of our cousins showed up. I still don't know how he found us, but he rang the doorbell and asked if he could stay with us, if we could hide him, because he was on the run. We'd been in Europe a while by then, and we hadn't had any news from back home, so we asked him to catch us up, tell us how everyone was doing, how our grandmother was coping. "She died", he told us. "Three years ago". She'd been dead for three years and we hadn't known. We thought she was still there, exactly where we'd left her, just a bit older, but instead she was already rotting underground. I think that was the moment my mother realised, for the first time, that even if she'd wanted to go back, she had no home to go back to.

THE BURLY ONE: What would your grandmother sing?

THE BEAUTIFUL ONE: Just some of our songs. Traditionals.

THE BURLY ONE: Do you remember any?

THE BEAUTIFUL ONE: Yes.

THE BURLY ONE: Sing for me.

THE BEAUTIFUL ONE: I don't feel like it.

THE BURLY ONE: I'm not asking.

THE BEAUTIFUL ONE begins to sing a traditional song. THE TALL ONE hums along. THE BURLY ONE takes out the hairbrush and brushes her hair as she sings.

SCENE TWO

*THE TALL ONE, THE BEAUTIFUL ONE and THE STOCKY ONE.
THE STOCKY ONE is asleep. THE BEAUTIFUL ONE is looking at some
photographs. THE TALL ONE approaches her.*

THE TALL ONE: Was that true? The story about the hairbrush?

THE BEAUTIFUL ONE: Not a word of it.

THE TALL ONE: Really?

THE BEAUTIFUL ONE: I found it in a flea market.

THE TALL ONE: The song was real, though?

THE BEAUTIFUL ONE: Yeah, that was. My mother used to sing it
when I was little.

THE TALL ONE notices the photo.

THE TALL ONE: Is that you and your boyfriend?

THE BEAUTIFUL ONE: Ex-boyfriend.

THE TALL ONE: Oh. I'm sorry.

THE BEAUTIFUL ONE: That's OK.

THE TALL ONE: I'm always making gaffes like that.

THE BEAUTIFUL ONE: It's because you ask so many questions.

THE TALL ONE: Well, I'm curious. (*pointing at the photo*) Where are
you in this?

THE BEAUTIFUL ONE: At the beach.

THE TALL ONE: On holiday?

THE BEAUTIFUL ONE: Yeah.

THE TALL ONE: So... no, forget it, I'll just make another gaffe.

THE BEAUTIFUL ONE: You're wondering how we afforded it? We weren't that poor. He came from a good family. I met him studying medicine.

THE TALL ONE: You studied medicine?

THE BEAUTIFUL ONE: Yeah. But I never managed to find a job as a doctor. He always said we'd have to look further afield, to leave. But I didn't want to.

THE TALL ONE: Why?

THE BEAUTIFUL ONE: I'd taken a while to settle down. To feel at home.

THE TALL ONE: Did he leave without you then?

THE BEAUTIFUL ONE: No, he was too in love with me. He would've taken a shit job, done anything, just to be able to stay with me.

THE TALL ONE: Why did you break up?

THE BEAUTIFUL ONE: He died.

THE TALL ONE: Fuck, I'm so sorry. I didn't mean to... I'm so sorry...

THE BEAUTIFUL ONE: We were crossing the road, I stopped to look in a shop window, he was always distracted, this truck skidded across and he didn't see it. This massive grey truck.

THE TALL ONE: I'm so sorry.

THE BEAUTIFUL ONE: Let's talk about something else, shall we? Tell me about you.

THE TALL ONE: Um, OK... well, I'm curious, prone to gaffes, I studied humanities because I thought, well, the economy's screwed, so what's the point studying something I hate to get a job I might not get? I might as well do something I like, right? But I'm not sure if I actually enjoyed it in the end. I'm still searching. I'm quite easy-going, sociable I like chocolate and... why did you decide to leave?

THE BEAUTIFUL ONE: You not worried about another gaffe?

THE TALL ONE: A bit.

THE BEAUTIFUL ONE: You know what you should do, instead of wasting time asking me questions?

THE TALL ONE: What?

THE BEAUTIFUL ONE: Pick up that suitcase and smash his head in with it while he sleeps.

THE TALL ONE: What?

THE BEAUTIFUL ONE: It's the only way you'll save yourself.

THE TALL ONE: What are you on about?

THE BEAUTIFUL ONE: Trust me.

THE TALL ONE: You're crazy.

THE BEAUTIFUL ONE: You've got to make sure you attack first. If you don't, I will.

THE TALL ONE: Oh, come on...

THE BEAUTIFUL ONE: Worried you'll get blood on your suitcase?

THE TALL ONE: No, but... would you really smash someone's head in while they sleep?

THE BEAUTIFUL ONE: Yes, so that he can't smash yours in as soon as you fall asleep.

THE TALL ONE: I don't understand, how do you... did you already know him?

THE BEAUTIFUL ONE: Never seen him in my life.

THE TALL ONE: So?

THE BEAUTIFUL ONE: I know how these things go.

THE TALL ONE: You'd kill him?

THE BEAUTIFUL ONE: Yes.

THE TALL ONE: To save me?

THE BEAUTIFUL ONE: I'd rather you did it.

THE TALL ONE: But if I don't, you will?

THE BEAUTIFUL ONE: Yes. Want to ask me again?

THE TALL ONE: No, but it's just... even if he's as dangerous as you say he is, why do you care? Wouldn't it be easier to just mind your own business?

THE BEAUTIFUL ONE: When one person is stronger and one is weaker, "minding my own business" means siding with the stronger. It's either you or him.

THE TALL ONE: And you chose me?

THE BEAUTIFUL ONE: Do you want me to choose him?

THE TALL ONE: No, no.

THE BEAUTIFUL ONE: Well, get on with it then.

THE TALL ONE: But he hasn't actually done anything to me. He just asked me for money. He hasn't threatened me, he hasn't...

THE BEAUTIFUL ONE: You've got five seconds, otherwise I'm doing it.

THE TALL ONE: Oh, come on.

Silence.

THE STOCKY ONE: Before anyone does anything stupid, I'm awake.

THE BEAUTIFUL ONE: See? You took too long.

THE STOCKY ONE: I've been awake the whole time.

THE BEAUTIFUL ONE: He was snoring

THE STOCKY ONE: I heard everything. Your boyfriend was run over by a truck. At least, that's what you say happened. The truth is you probably killed him in his sleep.

THE BEAUTIFUL ONE: (*to THE TALL ONE*) Now you're fucked.

THE TALL ONE: Me? I didn't want to do anything. It was you who... it was her.

THE STOCKY ONE: Yes, I heard. Don't blame her though. I get it. She's used to her own kind, she doesn't know we're more civilised here. We only use violence as a last resort.

THE BEAUTIFUL ONE glares at THE STOCKY ONE but refuses to rise to the bait. Refuses to give him the satisfaction.

The silence is incredibly uncomfortable.

THE TALL ONE: I... I don't think it's a question of/

THE STOCKY ONE: /Yes, yes, I know you fancy her. And she fancies you. You'll end up fucking and this container will become your little love nest, congratulations. But let's be clear: I'm a very light sleeper, so no funny business.

SCENE THREE

THE TALL ONE, THE STOCKY ONE and THE BEAUTIFUL ONE.
THE BEAUTIFUL ONE and THE STOCKY ONE are lying down, one on
each side of the container. THE TALL ONE is pacing, and looking around the
container. He lets out a deep sigh. He doesn't feel well.

THE STOCKY ONE: You're turning greener by the day. I thought
you'd got used to the seasickness.

THE TALL ONE: I don't think it's that.

THE STOCKY ONE: Claustrophobia?

THE BEAUTIFUL ONE: Does claustrophobia turn people green?

THE STOCKY ONE: Are you claustrophobic?

THE TALL ONE: I think so.

THE STOCKY ONE: What do you mean you 'think so'? Yes or no.

THE TALL ONE: I didn't think so, but now I'm realising I
probably am.

THE BEAUTIFUL ONE: And it makes you turn green?

THE TALL ONE: No, I don't think it's that either.

THE STOCKY ONE: What's wrong with you, then? You're
breathing all weird.

THE TALL ONE: I'm breathing perfectly fine, I just...

THE STOCKY ONE: What?

THE TALL ONE: I need a shit, OK? I've been holding it in for
two days but I can't hold it any longer.

THE STOCKY ONE: Right, well, we peed in that corner, just go
and do it there. Just be careful where you put your feet.

THE TALL ONE doesn't move.

24

THE BEAUTIFUL ONE: What's wrong?

THE TALL ONE: I don't know if I can go with you both watching me.

THE STOCKY ONE: Clearly you're not that desperate then.

THE TALL ONE: No, seriously, it's psychological.

THE STOCKY ONE: If you really needed to go, you'd be able to even if I was there staring you in the eyes.

THE BEAUTIFUL ONE: What if we turn around, would that work?

THE TALL ONE: Yes, please. Could you?

THE BEAUTIFUL ONE: Come on, let's turn around.

THE STOCKY ONE: Yeah, sure, I was only joking.

THE TALL ONE: Thanks.

THE TALL ONE disappears into the corner.

THE STOCKY ONE approaches THE BEAUTIFUL ONE.

THE STOCKY ONE: So, what are we gonna do?

THE BEAUTIFUL ONE: Look, can't you just take his money while he's asleep? Open his suitcase and just take it without hurting him.

THE STOCKY ONE: It's locked.

THE BEAUTIFUL ONE: Well, get the key.

THE STOCKY ONE: There is no key, it's a combination. And I'll give him the money back anyway. It's all true. Apart from the Audi, it's not an A7, it's an A5. Would you really have smashed my head in with the suitcase?

THE BEAUTIFUL ONE: Yes.

THE STOCKY ONE: Listen, if it gets violent, are you going to try and defend him?

THE BEAUTIFUL ONE: Yes.

THE STOCKY ONE: Then I'll have to hurt you too.

THE BEAUTIFUL ONE: You can try.

THE STOCKY ONE: Why don't you just not get involved?

THE BEAUTIFUL ONE: Are you scared, two against one?

THE STOCKY ONE: No. But it's a shame I'll have to ruin that pretty smile.

THE BEAUTIFUL ONE: I thought I was a dirty fucking immigrant who ruined your continent.

THE STOCKY ONE: Doesn't mean you can't have a pretty smile. Listen, just stay out of it, OK? It'll be over quickly. I've already tried with words. There's no other alternative.

THE BEAUTIFUL ONE: Everyone's entitled to their point of view.

THE STOCKY ONE: No deal, then?

THE BEAUTIFUL ONE: No.

THE STOCKY ONE: OK.

THE STOCKY ONE grabs THE BEAUTIFUL ONE by the throat, and begins to strangle her. She screams. THE TALL ONE approaches, his trousers still round his ankles.

THE TALL ONE: What's going on?

THE STOCKY ONE: It's perfectly simple. We've been at sea for several days. We could arrive any minute now. So now give me the money, or I'll kill her.

THE TALL ONE: How many times do I have to say it? I don't have any/

THE STOCKY ONE: /No, no, we've done enough talking already. Now listen to me. I'm in trouble. And trouble makes people desperate. Understood?

THE TALL ONE: Yes.

THE STOCKY ONE: So, I'll ask you again: will you lend me six hundred dollars?

THE TALL ONE: Wait, listen I know you don't want to talk anymore, but we have to. So let's try talking hypothetically.

THE STOCKY ONE: What the fuck are you on about?

THE TALL ONE: I'll tell you what I would say and you reply by saying what you would respond, but without actually talking or replying to each other. It's a way to avoid doing anything rash which we might later regret

THE STOCKY ONE: OK.

THE TALL ONE: OK. So, if I now said: "I'm really sorry to hear of your predicament, I empathise greatly with you, and I really hope you manage to get out of it, but I can't lend you six hundred dollars." What would you do?

THE STOCKY ONE: I'd tell you to stop taking the piss.

THE TALL ONE: "I'm not taking the piss".

THE STOCKY ONE: Are we still talking hypothetically or are you actually saying that?

THE TALL ONE: We're still talking hypothetically.

THE STOCKY ONE: At this point, then, hypothetically, I'd snap her neck. And then I'd turn on you.

THE TALL ONE: Why though?

THE STOCKY ONE: Because you're taking the piss.

THE TALL ONE: I'm not taking the piss.

THE STOCKY ONE: Yes you are.

THE TALL ONE: OK, fine, let's try this: what would I have to say to convince you that I'm not taking the piss out of you?

THE STOCKY ONE: You'd have to admit you don't want to give me the money.

THE TALL ONE: OK. I don't want to give you the money.

THE STOCKY ONE: So you do have it?

THE TALL ONE: No, I don't have it, I don't, I swear, but if I did I'd give it to you, not because I trust you, or because you've convinced me, or even because I give a fuck whether they kill you or not I'd give it to you because I'm scared of you. That's the only reason I'd give you the money. But I don't have it.

THE STOCKY ONE: Are we still talking hypothetically or are you actually saying this?

THE TALL ONE: I'm actually saying this.

THE STOCKY ONE: OK. I trust you.

THE TALL ONE: Really?

THE STOCKY ONE: Yes. But I want to check. Give me the combination to your suitcase.

THE TALL ONE: There's nothing in my suitcase.

THE STOCKY ONE: Tell me the combination or I'll kill her.

THE TALL ONE: I'm telling you, there's nothing in there.

THE STOCKY ONE: You're a piece of shit.

THE STOCKY ONE pushes THE BEAUTIFUL ONE away from him, without hurting her, moves towards THE TALL ONE and punches him.

THE TALL ONE tries to defend himself. There is a struggle, as THE STOCKY ONE tries to subdue THE TALL ONE. The struggle stops as a microphone falls from THE TALL ONE's pocket. It's on.

THE BEAUTIFUL ONE: What's that?

THE STOCKY ONE picks it up and looks at it.

THE STOCKY ONE: A microphone.

THE BEAUTIFUL ONE: A microphone?

THE STOCKY ONE: I think so.

THE TALL ONE: Yes, it's an audio recorder.

THE BEAUTIFUL ONE: What are you recording?

THE STOCKY ONE: Hey! She asked you a question: what are you recording? Are you police, a border guard, what are you?

THE TALL ONE: I'm a writer. I want to write a book. A piece of documentary fiction about...

THE BEAUTIFUL ONE: About?

THE TALL ONE: About the new emigrants.

THE BEAUTIFUL ONE: So you want to make money at our expense?

THE TALL ONE: No, it's not about money, I just want to tell the story/

THE BEAUTIFUL ONE: /That's why you were asking all of those questions. You wanted a few sad stories, didn't you? Lovely. What are we, just animals in a zoo for you then? Fancied a journey in a cage with us so you can go and tell everyone how dirty and evil we are?

THE TALL ONE: No, listen/

THE BEAUTIFUL ONE: /You know what's missing for your book? A few bruises. If you've got a phone we can take a few photos for the front cover.

THE TALL ONE: What are you suggesting?

THE BEAUTIFUL ONE: What am I suggesting? That I was trying to help you out and you were taking the piss.

THE TALL ONE: No, I'm not taking the piss out of anyone.

THE STOCKY ONE: It's not looking great, mate. Want me to defend you? That'll be six hundred dollars.

THE TALL ONE: I told you, I don't have it.

THE BEAUTIFUL ONE: You've got a thousand though, right?

THE TALL ONE: Yes, but I need that.

THE BEAUTIFUL ONE: Let's take the thousand.

THE TALL ONE: And then what will I do?

THE BEAUTIFUL ONE: Haven't you heard? Dead writers sell better.

THE TALL ONE: No, hold on/

THE STOCKY ONE: /Six hundred for me and four hundred for you?

THE BEAUTIFUL ONE: Great.

THE STOCKY ONE: Deal.

THE TALL ONE: No, wait a second, you don't understand. I didn't want to take advantage of you. I'm not just here to write my book, I'm emigrating too. I'm genuinely leaving. Like you. Please don't hurt me. I'm just like you.

THE BEAUTIFUL ONE: We're emigrating because we've got no other choice.

THE TALL ONE: Neither do I: I don't have a job, or a project, I have no opportunities. Yes, I could've stayed at my parents' house for another ten years, they would've taken care of me, they would've fed me, but what kind of life is that? What life would that have been? You don't realise, but you're lucky, because you're... how do I put this... in touch with life. Real life. I've always felt like there was some sort of filter, between me and real life. That's why I used this crisis as an opportunity. To change everything.

THE BEAUTIFUL ONE: You're ridiculous.

HE TALL ONE: I wanted to write about this journey, yes, but not to profit from your suffering. I wanted to tell people about it. About mine. Mine and yours. Maybe I should've told you, I was wrong, but I mean, I don't even know if they'll publish it. (*rambling*) I spoke with an editor who seemed interested and we've stayed in touch over email but it's not a given, nothing is certain, I can only hope. Just like you hope. Just like you.

THE STOCKY ONE: Where is this editor?

THE TALL ONE: In the place we're going.

THE BEAUTIFUL ONE: Which is secret.

THE TALL ONE: Not for me.

THE BEAUTIFUL ONE: Or for him, apparently. The only idiot who doesn't know what's going on is me.

THE TALL ONE: We can tell you where we're going, if you want. I didn't say earlier because I wasn't sure if... (*to THE STOCKY ONE*) Can we tell her?

THE STOCKY ONE: Do what you want.

THE TALL ONE: We're going to Japan.

THE STOCKY ONE: What the fuck are you on about?

THE TALL ONE: What? Where do you think we're going?

THE STOCKY ONE: Venezuela.

THE TALL ONE: Venezuela? Why would we go to Venezuela?

THE STOCKY ONE: That's where the future is..

THE TALL ONE: What future?

THE STOCKY ONE: That's my business. Anyway, I've got a driver waiting for me in Venezuela. We're headed there, you can forget about your fucking Japanese editor.

THE TALL ONE: Who told you we're going to Venezuela?

THE STOCKY ONE: Our friend from earlier.

THE TALL ONE: He was lying to you.

THE STOCKY ONE: How do you know he wasn't lying to you?

THE BEAUTIFUL ONE: He lied to both of you. All three of us. He told me we were going to Australia.

THE STOCKY ONE: Fucking hell. Oi, bastard. You bastard, where are you? I'll smash your container up! I will! I will fucking kick it in. And then I'll kick your fucking head in. Yeah? You better hope we're headed to Venezuela, otherwise you're fucked. You're fucked, you get me? You're fucked!

A loud bang. The lighting begins to flicker, and we hear waves hitting against the side of the container.

SCENE FOUR

THE BURLY ONE.

THE BURLY ONE: The term shipwreck denotes the total submersion of a ship or boat by accidental causes. Acts of war are thus excluded, for which the term "sinking" is generally used instead. The main causes of shipwreck are the following. A failure or loss in the hull, which can cause flooding and therefore a lack of hydrostatic thrust. This is particularly common in wooden boats. Instability – if the distribution of weight moves the centre of mass, moves the metacentre, the boat may tilt sideways. Navigational error – many accidents occur as a direct result of crew error, which may include failing to avoid collision with rocks, other ships, or icebergs, as in the famous case of the Titanic. Meteorological events - weather conditions which are dangerous for navigation include strong winds, reduced visibility due to fog, or intense old. Marine attacks – although rare, there are historical cases of sinkings caused by marine wildlife attack, as seems to have been the case for the American whaling ship Essex. With an average ocean temperature of about fifteen degrees, the survival time of a castaway exposed to ocean currents is approximately three hours and forty-two minutes. (*He turns to the other three*) Here comes the storm. Hold on tight and try not to hit your head. And, if you really have to die, don't dent my container.

ACT THREE – THE CONTAINER AT SEA

SCENE ONE

THE TALL ONE and THE BEAUTIFUL ONE are lying down, leaning against THE TALL ONE's suitcase.

THE STOCKY ONE is standing, tired. He looks around, looks out to sea, unsure what to do. After a while THE TALL ONE opens his eyes and sits up.

THE TALL ONE: What happened?

THE STOCKY ONE: A storm. The container flipped over and you both hit your heads.

THE TALL ONE: Is she dead?

THE STOCKY ONE: No. She's breathing.

THE TALL ONE: How did we not drown?

THE STOCKY ONE: I opened the container and pulled you out. I held onto your suitcase and dragged you up here.

THE TALL ONE: Right. So what now? We've got to alert the coastguard. Don't we have a phone, a flare, anything? One of those things that what happened to the ship? And all the people? Did no one... why is this container floating?

THE STOCKY ONE: It's made of wood.

THE TALL ONE: It looks like it's metal.

THE STOCKY ONE: It's plated. But it's wooden underneath. See? The casing has ripped off. That prick didn't even have the money to buy himself a proper container.

THE TALL ONE: So, is nothing left? Isn't there a phone onboard, something to broadcast an SOS? Where's the big guy? What happened to him?

THE STOCKY ONE: I'm sorry, I didn't notice, I was too busy saving myself, and trying to save you.

THE TALL ONE: Sorry.

THE STOCKY ONE: What's the code for your suitcase?

THE TALL ONE: What?

THE STOCKY ONE: I tried to open it but couldn't.

THE TALL ONE: Are you still on about money? What good is money now that...

THE STOCKY ONE: I was looking for some dry clothes. Given it was floating I assume it's also waterproof.

THE TALL ONE: Yes, it's waterproof.

THE STOCKY ONE: It'll get dark soon, and we'll freeze if we're still wearing wet clothes.

THE TALL ONE: You're right. It's already freezing I'll open it. Wait, there's a computer in there too, maybe it'll find some sort of network, come on

THE TALL ONE opens the suitcase, pulls out his computer and turns it on.

In the meantime, THE STOCKY ONE pulls out a shirt and puts it on. He pulls another out for THE BEAUTIFUL ONE and approaches her.

THE STOCKY ONE: Wake up.

He slaps the sides of her face, trying to bring her round.

THE STOCKY ONE: Wake up. You've got to change otherwise you'll freeze.

THE BEAUTIFUL ONE opens her eyes.

THE BEAUTIFUL ONE: What happened?

35

THE STOCKY ONE: A storm. We're shipwrecked. But we're OK. The ship sank, the container is floating because it's made of wood. You need to put these clothes on, otherwise you'll freeze.

THE STOCKY ONE hands her the clothes, then goes back over to THE TALL ONE.

THE STOCKY ONE: So?

THE TALL ONE: There's no signal.

THE STOCKY ONE: How's the battery?

THE TALL ONE: Low.

THE STOCKY ONE: Keep it switched off. We'll try again in a bit. Maybe if we move with the current we'll find a spot with some signal.

THE TALL ONE: We're going to die here, aren't we? No one's looking for us, no one knows we exist. If we were near a coastline but no, of course not, we're in the middle of the ocean. Not a single other human in sight. Fucking hell. I don't believe it. I don't want to die of hunger in the middle of the ocean.

Panicking, he starts to shout.

THE TALL ONE: Heeeeelp!

THE STOCKY ONE: What are you doing?

THE TALL ONE: I'm shouting. Heeeeelp! Heeeeelp! Can anyone hear me? We're here! We're heeeeere!

THE STOCKY ONE: Don't waste your energy.

THE TALL ONE: Why the fuck not? Why? Even if I waste my energy how does that change anything? I don't want to die of hunger at sea. Do you get that?

In the meantime, THE BEAUTIFUL ONE has sat up and is putting on the shirt.

THE BEAUTIFUL ONE: You'll die of thirst first.

THE TALL ONE: What?

THE BEAUTIFUL ONE: You'll die of thirst before you die of hunger.

THE TALL ONE: How long does it take?

THE BEAUTIFUL ONE: Two or three days.

THE TALL ONE: Can't we drink seawater?

THE STOCKY ONE: No.

THE TALL ONE: Why?

THE STOCKY ONE: Because you can't.

THE TALL ONE: What kind of answer is that?

THE BEAUTIFUL ONE: You can't drink seawater because it's too salty.

THE TALL ONE: So? It might taste bad but at least we won't die.

THE BEAUTIFUL ONE: It'll make us die faster. Our kidneys can't filter it, it contains too much salt. So instead of quenching your thirst, it makes it worse.

THE STOCKY ONE: We've got to collect rainwater. Let's use your suitcase, we'll empty it, leave it open and hope it rains.

THE TALL ONE: What if it doesn't?

THE STOCKY ONE: We'll drink our own piss.

THE TALL ONE: I have a bottle of water.

THE STOCKY ONE: Right. You gonna keep it to yourself, or share it with us?

THE TALL ONE: We can share it.

THE TALL ONE pulls a bottle of water out of his suitcase.

THE BEAUTIFUL ONE: Thanks.

THE STOCKY ONE: When we've drunk it all we can start pissing in the bottle.

THE TALL ONE: I can't wait.

THE BEAUTIFUL ON: Come on, put a dry shirt on, now.

THE TALL ONE puts on a dry shirt. THE STOCKY ONE looks around and finds a piece of wood.

THE TALL ONE: So how long before we die of hunger?

THE BEAUTIFUL ONE: Oh, a month, maybe more? That is, if we had water and we weren't already exhausted.

THE TALL ONE: So?

THE STOCKY ONE: Both of you, give me your shoelaces.

THE TALL ONE: Are you going to hang yourself?

THE STOCKY ONE: I'm going to try to make a fishing line. Look in your pockets. See if you've got any crumbs of anything to use as bait.

THE TALL ONE: How will we cook the fish?

THE STOCKY ONE: Well, you wanted to go to Japan, don't you like sushi?

THE TALL ONE: Not really.

THE STOCKY ONE: You might have to get used to it.

THE TALL ONE: What if you don't catch anything?

THE STOCKY ONE: You got any better ideas? Otherwise shut up and give me your laces.

THE STOCKY ONE takes the shoelaces, moves off into the corner and tries to fish.

THE TALL ONE and THE BEAUTIFUL ONE stay where they are, close together. Some time passes. The sun comes up and warms them.

THE TALL ONE: Why did you want to go to Australia?

THE BEAUTIFUL ONE: Do you want to take notes while I answer?

THE TALL ONE: I'm just trying to make conversation.

THE BEAUTIFUL ONE: Well, you say something then.

THE TALL ONE: What's got into you?

THE BEAUTIFUL ONE: I don't want to end up in some stupid book. If we even survive, that is.

THE TALL ONE: Weren't you listening before? I said that I'm not/

THE BEAUTIFUL ONE: /I don't care. Don't try to convince me. If you want to talk to me, talk about something else. Otherwise, pray. Do you believe in God?

THE TALL ONE: No. You?

THE BEAUTIFUL ONE: I think so. Sometimes not.

THE TALL ONE: I didn't intend to profit from what's going on here. At all. I just wanted to offer a story of hope, of rebirth. Sure, there would've been some cultural criticism, some commentary on current affairs, but all with the aim of encouraging hope in the future. Our future. Mine and yours, all of us on this desperate journey, suffering together, so that we can/

THE BEAUTIFUL ONE: /Die at sea.

THE TALL ONE: I hope not. I can't even imagine that.

THE BEAUTIFUL ONE: You're full of shit.

THE TALL ONE: Why?

THE BEAUTIFUL ONE: Because no one who's suffering wants people to share their story. They want to forget it. People like you think you're helping by telling people our sad stories. The pain, the exploitation, the trauma – you use it all for 'social commentary'. To condemn, to criticise. But we just want to leave it all behind.

THE TALL ONE: But do you think that's right? Do you think it's right that people are forced to cross the sea in shipping containers?

THE BEAUTIFUL ONE: No.

THE TALL ONE: Then it has to be written about. The story has to be told. Saying nothing is the same as saying you're fine with it. How can you not agree? You wanted to kill him to defend me.

THE BEAUTIFUL ONE: I was wrong.

THE TALL ONE: But you had an opinion.

THE BEAUTIFUL ONE: You know what the difference is between us? I wanted to save someone. You want people with enough money to buy a book, and enough time to read it, to say "oh look how good this young writer is, he's produced such a socially conscious piece". Well, fuck you.

THE TALL ONE: So, the problem is that I'm not desperate enough? If I were more desperate it'd all be fine?

THE BEAUTIFUL ONE: The problem is that you're not truthful.

THE TALL ONE: But the book I wanted to write/

THE BEAUTIFUL ONE: /The book you wanted to write is a pile of shit. Because it's a lie. You know what your problem is? You don't appreciate what you've got. If I had a home, with someone who loved me, then fuck social commentary and criticism. I'd write poems. Songs. I'd only write beautiful things.

THE TALL ONE: Beautiful things aren't interesting.

THE BEAUTIFUL ONE: Just because you're not interested in them doesn't mean they're not interesting. I'm interested in them.

THE STOCKY ONE: I've caught something. It's small but it's moving.

THE TALL ONE and THE BEAUTIFUL ONE approach THE STOCKY ONE and gather round him.

THE STOCKY ONE pulls something out of the water: it is THE BEAUTIFUL ONE's wooden hairbrush.

THE BEAUTIFUL ONE: My hairbrush.

THE TALL ONE: Just as well it was moving.

THE STOCKY ONE: If you don't like my fishing, you do it.

THE TALL ONE: Well, it's not your fault, you just haven't caught anything yet.

THE STOCKY ONE: Well, there aren't any fucking fish left.

THE TALL ONE: Maybe deeper there are.

THE STOCKY ONE: Oh I'm sorry, I left my deep sea fishing rod at home.

THE TALL ONE: Why do you take everything so personally?

THE STOCKY ONE: Why do you never have anything intelligent to say?

THE TALL ONE: That was intelligent.

THE STOCKY ONE: But it wasn't appropriate. If you say something intelligent in the wrong context it's no longer intelligent, it's stupid.

THE TALL ONE: Fine, whatever you say.

THE BEAUTIFUL ONE: I think this hairbrush is a sign from fate. It's my grandmother sending us a message.

THE STOCKY ONE: Great. Superstition is the last thing we need.

THE TALL ONE: So, it is your grandmother's hairbrush?

THE BEAUTIFUL ONE: Yeah.

THE TALL ONE: So, the story you told the big guy was true?

THE BEAUTIFUL ONE: Partly.

THE STOCKY ONE: What does your religion say? That if a woman finds a hairbrush in the sea it means the coastguard's on its way?

THE TALL ONE: Hey, can you just not –

THE STOCKY ONE: Why don't you fuck off?

THE TALL ONE: I would if I could.

THE TALL ONE walks away and sits on the other side of the container, facing away. THE BEAUTIFUL ONE and THE STOCKY ONE stay where they are.

THE STOCKY ONE: I'll never catch anything with this.

THE BEAUTIFUL ONE: No, you won't.

THE STOCKY ONE: Well, I guess if we don't want die of hunger before help arrives, then/

THE TALL ONE: /What?

THE STOCKY ONE: I thought you'd fucked off.

THE TALL ONE: I have. But I can still hear you.

THE STOCKY ONE: Good for you.

THE TALL ONE: So? If the coastguard doesn't find us, what?

THE STOCKY ONE: You know.

THE TALL ONE: No, I don't know. We'll have to drink our own piss? You've already said that, but I still hope it's going to rain. If it doesn't, I'll drink my piss, I'll drink my own piss so I don't die, ok?

THE BEAUTIFUL ONE: I know what you were going to say.

THE TALL ONE: What? What do you know? Come on, tell me: what's this amazing thing you've understood that I haven't?

THE BEAUTIFUL ONE: That to avoid dying of hunger, the only food left in this container is us.

THE STOCKY ONE: And the only liquid left is our blood.

THE BEAUTIFUL ONE: But there's still time.

SCENE TWO

THE BURLY ONE.

THE BURLY ONE: Existing human knowledge suggests that time
   began when the universe began. Observable material and
   spatial changes regulated by physics determine the passing
   of time. All entities which move or change in space can
   also be described in terms of time. Two of the most notable
   examples of the correlation between time and motion are
   the rotation of the Earth around its axis, which determines
   night and day, and the path of its elliptical orbit around the
   sun, which determines the seasons. Our perception of time
   stems from the realization that reality, of which we are part,
   has materially changed. If I observe the different positions
   assumed by an ant moving across a table, if I pay attention
   to the succession of my thoughts or the beating of my heart
   – physiological and physical facts – I can conclude that a
   period of time has passed. The standard unit of measurement
   of time, according to the International System, is the
   "second". Based on this, broader measures are defined such as
   the minute, the hour, the day, the week, the month, the year,
   the half-decade, the decade, the century and the millennium.
   The instruments used for measuring time are named clocks.
   Highly accurate clocks are called chronometers.

SCENE THREE

THE TALL ONE, THE STOCKY ONE and THE BEAUTIFUL ONE are lying down, covered with clothes, exhausted. THE BEAUTIFUL ONE is looking at a photo.

THE TALL ONE: Your photos survived?

THE BEAUTIFUL ONE: Just this one. The others sank with my bag.

THE TALL ONE: Thank God it rained.

THE STOCKY ONE: You've already said that. And since you said it, it's stopped raining.

THE TALL ONE: I thought you didn't believe in superstition?

THE STOCKY ONE: I'm ready to believe in anything now.

THE BEAUTIFUL ONE: How much time do you think has passed?

THE TALL ONE: Three days? Five? I don't know.

THE BEAUTIFUL ONE: I feel like we've been here forever.

THE STOCKY ONE: We need to make sure we keep drinking.

THE TALL ONE: There's some piss left in the bottle. I think it's mine, you can have it.

THE STOCKY ONE: There isn't enough.

THE TALL ONE: I haven't been able to go for two days.

THE STOCKY ONE: We have to eat as well. I know you don't want to hear it, but it's true. We don't have long left.

THE TALL ONE: I don't feel like I'm about to die.

THE STOCKY ONE: When you feel like you're about to die, it'll be too late. We'll lose consciousness. We've got to do something whilst we're still lucid, and/

THE TALL ONE: /And ?

THE STOCKY ONE: And we've still got enough strength.

THE TALL ONE: Listen, I get what you're saying, but my answer is no. I won't even think about it, absolutely not. Plus, even if we decided to I can't even say it.

THE STOCKY ONE: To eat.

THE TALL ONE: Right, to eat.

THE STOCKY ONE: One of us.

THE TALL ONE: Even if we wanted to – and I don't want to – who would we eat?

THE BEAUTIFUL ONE: Why, if we don't pick you will you change your mind?

THE TALL ONE: No. I just mean we're never going to agree anyway. So we either all fight to try and kill each other, or we forget about it. I say we forget about it.

THE STOCKY ONE: Well, I've been thinking about this for a while, actually. The most obvious choice would be for the two of us to team up and eat her, because she's the weakest. But she's also the only woman left, so no. We've got to pick between the two of us, and I think we should pick the one who deserves it the most, the biggest twat, which is you.

THE TALL ONE: Hang on, I don't understand that argument at all.

THE BEAUTIFUL ONE: Why not me?

THE STOCKY ONE: Do you want to be eaten?

THE BEAUTIFUL ONE: And what do you mean by "only woman left"? As if I were some sort of raw material. What would you do once it's just the two of us?

THE STOCKY ONE: Fine, let's consider all of us. He's still the biggest twat though, so I'd pick him. Happy?

THE BEAUTIFUL ONE: Well, why shouldn't we pick you?

THE TALL ONE: Yeah: why not you?

THE STOCKY ONE: Because you deserve it.

THE TALL ONE: Who says? You're the reason businesses failed, you were accused of bankruptcy fraud, and then you flee to Venezuela, you or maybe those were all lies to try and get my money. That's even worse.

THE STOCKY ONE: You would've left me for dead just to get a more interesting story for your book.

THE TALL ONE: What?

THE STOCKY ONE: You don't think I know that? That's why you didn't want to give me the money.

THE TALL ONE: Are you still on about the money? I don't have ittttttttt! Why do we have to eat the biggest twat? Why don't we eat the biggest fucking moron, which is you. Anyway, why do we have to pick who to eat based on these stupid arguments? Let's pull a name out of a hat, that'd be better. If we really have to do this actually... no, no. I got carried away – I am not doing this. Absolutely not. Fucking hell, I don't want to eat you, I'm not a cannibal, you're both out of your minds, I don't want to eat anyone. I'd prefer us all to die of hunger.

THE STOCKY ONE: Great, so we'll eat you then. If you want to die anyway.

THE TALL ONE: I want to die so I don't have to eat you, not so I get eaten by you.

THE STOCKY ONE: Well, what's the difference? Once you're dead you won't know what happens to you.

THE TALL ONE: But I know now, and I'm saying no.

THE STOCKY ONE: Well, you're an idiot. You've decided you're going to die anyway.

THE TALL ONE: I haven't decided to die, I said that if we have to die, I will die.

THE STOCKY ONE: What's the difference?

THE TALL ONE: Well, we might die in ten days' time. And you want to kill me now. To eat me. And drink my blood.

THE STOCKY ONE: To at least try to save me and her. If you want to die anyway.

THE TALL ONE: But I don't want to die to save you. Once I'm dead I won't care what happens to you.

THE STOCKY ONE: See? So selfish.

THE TALL ONE: Selfish? Well, why don't you let us eat you then, if you're so selfless.

THE STOCKY ONE: Would you eat me?

THE TALL ONE: No! I won't eat you! Plus, how would we – like, mouthfuls? Just raw? What are we talking about here?

THE STOCKY ONE: See you're just confirming it, we've got to eat you.

THE TALL ONE: Well, sorry, I'm not happy with that.

THE STOCKY ONE: It's not up to you.

THE TALL ONE: No?

THE STOCKY ONE: Majority rules.

THE TALL ONE: Well, when did we decide that?

THE STOCKY ONE: That's how democracy works.

THE TALL ONE: Don't start lecturing me on democracy.

THE STOCKY ONE: Even if one citizen doesn't want to vote, the others can.

THE TALL ONE: Yes, but in the real world, that citizen can leave, and go to a different country. They're not stuck on a fucking container with two people who are trying to eat him.

THE BEAUTIFUL ONE: Eat me. I'm tired. We make this big song and dance about surviving, but is surviving really that important?

Silence.

THE STOCKY ONE: We can eat a piece of each of us.

THE TALL ONE: A piece? What do you mean a piece?

THE STOCKY ONE: Like a non-vital part of the body. A hand, an ear, a chunk of thigh. We don't have a knife though.

THE TALL ONE: (*relieved*) Right! We don't have a knife. Shame. We need a knife. We'd need a knife to kill one of us and eat them, so...

THE STOCKY ONE: Well, we could just strangle them.

THE TALL ONE: You would strangle me?

THE STOCKY ONE: Yeah.

THE TALL ONE: And then you would just bite into me? My raw flesh?

THE STOCKY ONE: Well, don't think I don't think it's gross.

THE TALL ONE: Clearly I find it more gross.

THE BEAUTIFUL ONE: I've told you, you can eat me.

THE TALL ONE: But it's not right.

THE BEAUTIFUL ONE: How do you know what's right and what's wrong?

THE TALL ONE: Well, I don't want to.

THE BEAUTIFUL ONE: It's not just up to you.

THE TALL ONE: I don't even want to talk about this anymore.

THE STOCKY ONE: Maybe we could start with our ears. Bite them off with our teeth.

THE TALL ONE: Well, let's start with yours then.

THE STOCKY ONE: We'd chosen you.

THE TALL ONE: I don't want anyone biting my ears. I'd rather you tried to strangle me. But I promise you, I'll defend myself as best I can. I'll defend myself till the last.

THE TALL ONE gets ready to fight. THE STOCKY ONE and THE BEAUTIFUL ONE don't move.

Suddenly THE BURLY ONE emerges from the sea and climbs onto the container.

THE BURLY ONE: Water. D'you have any water?

THE TALL ONE: Where have you come from?

THE BURLY ONE: I grabbed onto a piece of driftwood. Then I fainted. I didn't think anyone else had survived. I opened the container, before the ship sank.

THE STOCKY ONE: It sprang open by itself.

THE BURLY ONE: It was me. It's thanks to me that you're all still alive.

THE BEAUTIFUL ONE: And how are you still alive?

THE BURLY ONE: I had a bottle of water, but it's finished. Do you have any? Just a drop.

THE TALL ONE: Do you have any way of alerting the coastguard? A phone, a flare, anything.

THE BURLY ONE: Please, I'm dying of thirst.

THE STOCKY ONE: Where was the ship going?

THE BURLY ONE: What?

THE STOCKY ONE: Where were we going? You told each of us a different destination, but we must've been going somewhere.

THE BEAUTIFUL ONE: Why do you care anymore?

THE STOCKY ONE: I just want to know.

THE BURLY ONE: I can barely speak.

THE STOCKY ONE: I just need the name of a country.

THE BURLY ONE: Give me some water first.

THE STOCKY ONE hits THE BURLY ONE.

THE STOCKY ONE: Don't fuck me around. There's lots of ways of killing an animal, and some are very painful.

THE BURLY ONE: I didn't have any other option. You all wanted to go to different places.

THE TALL ONE: Well, we could have spoken about it. Maybe there would've been a solution that suited everyone. If you'd told us the truth/

THE BURLY ONE: /There's never a solution that works for everyone, didn't your parents teach you that? You were all screwed, and you needed to get away. Any place would do.

THE STOCKY ONE: Not for me. In Venezuela/

THE BURLY ONE: /In Venezuela what? You can chat your shit with them, but not with me. Where is the water? If you don't give me some I'll take it myself.

THE BURLY ONE moves, but THE STOCKY ONE hits him and holds him still.

THE STOCKY ONE: I've got an empire in Venezuela, OK? An empire. And thanks to you I'm here dying at sea with these two. We were talking about eating each other. Well, I think we've found a better solution now, haven't we? Easy. (*indicates THE BURLY ONE*) Plenty of flesh and blood to go around.

THE BEAUTIFUL ONE: Fine by me.

THE TALL ONE: I still don't agree, as a matter of principle. But I wouldn't stop you.

THE STOCKY ONE: If you tell me where the ship was headed I won't make you suffer. I'll break your neck in one movement – I know how – you just stay still, and you won't feel anything. Not that you deserve it.

THE BURLY ONE: They came looking for you, you know? Your "friends", the people you're running from. I told them I hadn't seen you. I saved your arse. People like us have to help each other out, otherwise we're fucked. So cut out all this shit about your empire in Venezuela and look at me: I'm just like you. We'll never be rich, or qualified, or well off, or have an empire in Venezuela. We're dirt poor, but we survive. You and I know how to survive.

THE STOCKY ONE: They weren't looking for me.

THE BURLY ONE: What?

THE STOCKY ONE: It was someone else.

THE BURLY ONE: Don't be pathetic.

THE STOCKY ONE: You know nothing about me

THE STOCKY ONE hits THE BURLY ONE. THE BURLY ONE defends himself and pushes him back.

THE BURLY ONE: I've got no energy left, neither do you. Don't be an idiot. There's no point trying to kill me. Let's kill him, that'd be way easier. I'll hold him still, you break his neck. Then we'll deal with her. Wouldn't that be better?

Silence.

THE STOCKY ONE: See, I don't get why you keep talking to me like a mate. I'm not your mate. (*He hits him*). I'm nothing like you. (*He hits him*). Do you get that? (*He hits him again, several times, and then grabs him by the neck*). I'm only in this fucking container because I got stuck in Europe without a visa, otherwise I would've left on a red carpet, you get me? A red carpet. And in Venezuela, when I walk around, people know me. They respect me. Not fucking pricks like you, real important people. I've got a villa with a pool and a fucking sea view. And when I get out of here – because I will, you've tried to ruin everything but you failed, I'm not going to die, do you get that, I am not going to die in your shipping container, I will get out of here, I'll sit there with a fucking cocktail and a woman either side of me, people'll walk past and look up and think "wow, what a lucky guy". But it's not luck. It's determination. It's determination that leads to success. It's determination that makes people like me different from people like you. And now I'm going to kill you like the animal you are.

THE STOCKY ONE starts strangling THE BURLY ONE. THE BURLY ONE is about to die when he pulls the knife out of his pocket at the last minute and stabs THE STOCKY ONE in the stomach.

THE STOCKY ONE slowly dies. THE BURLY ONE threatens the others with the knife.

THE BURLY ONE: Water. Give me water. And then dance for me. If you want to eat, you've got to dance for me. Both of you, at the same time. Something classical, I don't want any contemporary shit. And if I like it, I'll let you eat. If I don't, I won't.

ACT FOUR – EPILOGUE

SCENE ONE

THE BURLY ONE, THE TALL ONE, THE BEAUTIFUL ONE, and THE STOCKY ONE's body.

THE BURLY ONE has cut up THE STOCKY ONE and collected his blood in the suitcase and in the plastic bottle, which he is holding.

THE BURLY ONE: I understand if you're upset. We always get attached to people who've died. But it's pointless. Much better to think: rather him than me. But I know it's not easy, empathy creeps in. The term empathy was coined by Robert Vischer, scholar of aesthetics and figurative arts, in the late 1800s. The term emerged in the context of aesthetic study, in which empathy denotes fuck this. Life is fucking shit. It drives you insane. D'you know what I do to stop myself going insane? I eat. Every time I come back from a trip, I eat. I go into a fast food place and order two or three meals, then I go to a restaurant and spend all my money on meat, pasta, chips, desserts. I eat and eat, I get drunk on food, until my stomach hurts and I feel like I could explode, and just at that moment when it feels like my belly is going to tear open I finally feel alright in this shithole world. And then I faint. (*He passes the bottle to THE BEAUTIFUL ONE*). Here you go. You don't need to dance.

THE BEAUTIFUL ONE: Thanks.

THE BEAUTIFUL ONE drinks, then offers the bottle to THE TALL ONE.

THE TALL ONE: No.

THE BEAUTIFUL ONE: You've got to. Take the bottle.

THE TALL ONE: I don't even want to look at it.

THE BEAUTIFUL ONE: Let's have another hypothetical conversation. What will happen if you don't drink? You'll die. So you'd better drink.

THE TALL ONE: I thought you didn't care about staying alive.

THE BEAUTIFUL ONE: Well, you do.

THE TALL ONE: And you don't?

THE BEAUTIFUL ONE: It's different for me.

THE TALL ONE: It's always different for you. I can't stand you.

THE BEAUTIFUL ONE: I'm just trying to help you.

THE TALL ONE: You've been trying to help me since we met. We've never been able to have a normal conversation because you've always been trying to help me. All because I had some well-folded shirts? Even now, we're completely fucked, and you're still acting as if you're better, as if you're trying to "help" me. What the fuck do you want me to say? You emigrated and your partner died? I'm sorry, these things happen all the time, all around the world. Not everyone acts like they're better than everyone else just because they've suffered more.

THE BEAUTIFUL ONE: I know you're not well right now, but/

THE TALL ONE: /Fuck you. Don't patronize me. D'you think I want to die? NO. But I also don't want to drink blood from a plastic bottle that used to be full of piss. Do you even see what's happening? There's a dead body in my suitcase, blood everywhere... How can you both... what the fuck?! You're both animals, you're cannibals. I don't even know how to... What am I doing here with these fucking animals?! My father was right. Dad, you were right all along. I should've just stayed at home, now look where I've... you fucking disgust me. I find you disgusting. (*To THE STOCKY ONE's body or severed limbs*) And you? You wanted six hundred dollars? You need six hundred dollars? (*he grabs his suitcase, lifts up a false bottom and pulls out a plastic bag full of bank notes. He begins throwing notes onto THE*

STOCKY ONE's body). There you go. Six hundred, a thousand, two thousand. Do you know why my suitcase is waterproof? Because I used it when I travelled on my yacht. That's right, my parents have a fucking yacht. Here, that's twenty thousand, take it all, it's all yours. (*He throws the banknotes into the air, around the container, into the sea*). You can borrow all of it, it's yours. What you going to do with it now? You fucking bastard, what you gonna do with it?

THE TALL ONE grabs the bottle. He holds it and stares at it. Then he shuts his eyes, but keeps holding it without moving. He stays like that for a few seconds, then takes a gulp. Once he has swallowed the first gulp, he starts drinking more quickly, his eyes still shut. As he drinks, he cries. The more he drinks, the more he cries.

THE BURLY ONE: Hey, that's enough. Don't finish it all.

THE BURLY ONE takes the bottle back and puts it down. THE TALL ONE calms down. THE BEAUTIFUL ONE approaches him.

THE BEAUTIFUL ONE: (*amused*) Wow. Sorry.

THE TALL ONE: For what?

THE BEAUTIFUL ONE: Clearly I made my mind up too quickly about you.

THE TALL ONE: Yeah, well, you were right. I've been a twat.

THE BEAUTIFUL ONE: Yeah. You have. But you've also been quite... stoical.

THE TALL ONE: When?

THE BEAUTIFUL ONE: From the start.

THE TALL ONE: Have I?

THE BEAUTIFUL ONE: You didn't let it all get to you. Till now.

THE TALL ONE: Yeah, well. That was stupid of me.

THE BEAUTIFUL ONE: Stupid. Brave. My boyfriend could be like that too sometimes. I'm still not used to living without him. But here I am.

THE TALL ONE: I'm sorry for what I just said. I'm losing my mind.

THE BEAUTIFUL ONE nods.

THE BEAUTIFUL ONE: Someone will find us sooner or later, you'll see. They'll save us and we'll go off and live our lives. I'll move to Australia, or New Zealand. Not to Auckland or Wellington, to some little town, with nothing going on, no traffic. The white New Zealand culture is so young, did you know that? Apart from rugby, there are very few traditions. It's easier to integrate. I'll open my own bar, where people can come in, leave, have a coffee, say hello and you'll write an amazing book, and it'll be incredibly successful and sell millions of copies. And one day I'll come to visit you, wherever you're living: you'll hear the doorbell ring and you'll open the door and I'll be there to surprise you. And we'll hug, and greet each other, like two siblings that haven't seen each other for years. Here. (*She hands him the hairbrush*). It's a gift.

THE TALL ONE: Was it actually your grandmother's?

THE BEAUTIFUL ONE: Now it's yours.

THE TALL ONE: If we survive, I promise I won't write a single line about this journey.

THE BEAUTIFUL ONE: You can, if you want.

THE TALL ONE: No. I want to write poetry.

A brief silence in which he pulls out his computer and flips it open.

THE TALL ONE: I've got signal! I've got signal. I don't believe it. Maybe it's a satellite. We've got to send a message. We've got to send a message to someone.

THE BURLY ONE: Let's see.

THE BURLY ONE takes the computer from THE TALL ONE.

THE TALL ONE: What are you doing?

THE BURLY ONE: There's no signal.

THE TALL ONE: There was a second ago.

THE BEAUTIFUL ONE: There isn't.

THE TALL ONE: I swear there was just a second ago.

THE TALL ONE moves around holding the computer, looking for signal. The other two watch him. Suddenly, he stops and closes the computer.

THE BEAUTIFUL ONE: What happened?

THE TALL ONE: The battery's died. We're fucked. Wow, I really didn't think it would end like this.

THE BEAUTIFUL ONE: It won't.

THE TALL ONE: You're just saying that to make me feel better.

THE BEAUTIFUL ONE: I'm saying it because I hope it's true.

THE TALL ONE gets his audio recorder back out and looks at it. He turns it on.

THE TALL ONE'S RECORDED VOICE: We're setting sail tomorrow. I'm so excited. This will finally be the journey that I/

/THE TALL ONE switches it off. THE BEAUTIFUL ONE hugs him. A long silence. THE BURLY ONE suddenly points out to sea.

THE BURLY ONE: Look! A ship.

THE BEAUTIFUL ONE: What? I can't see anything.

THE TALL ONE: Me neither.

THE BURLY ONE: There's a ship, a big grey ship.

THE BEAUTIFUL ONE: Where?

THE BURLY ONE: Right out there.

THE BEAUTIFUL ONE: I can't see it.

THE TALL ONE: Me neither.

THE BEAUTIFUL ONE: Wait, yes. There is, there's something out there.

THE TALL ONE: What? Where?

THE BEAUTIFUL ONE: There. That grey speck on the water. It's a ship. It's a big ship coming right towards us.

THE TALL ONE: We've got to light a fire. We've got to make sure they see us. How? (*a thought*). The clothes, let's set fire to the clothes. Do you have a match? How do we start a fire?

THE BEAUTIFUL ONE: Wait, it's not a ship. It's too...

THE BURLY ONE: It's definitely a ship.

THE BEAUTIFUL ONE: No.

THE TALL ONE: What is it then?

THE BEAUTIFUL ONE: It looks like a whale.

THE TALL ONE: A whale?

THE BURLY ONE: A whale?! I'm telling you, it's a ship.

THE BEAUTIFUL ONE: No, I'm sure of it, it's definitely a whale. Look, it's moving up and down, it can't be a ship.

THE TALL ONE: You're right, it's moving in and out of the water.

THE BURLY ONE: What's a whale doing here?

THE TALL ONE: I imagine it's asking itself what a container is doing here.

THE BURLY ONE: It's not a whale. I'm telling you, it's a ship. It's a fucking ship. It's moving up and down on the waves. It's a ship.

THE TALL ONE: No, it's definitely a whale.

THE BEAUTIFUL ONE: Wait, it's not a single... there's more than one. Over there, look. Ten, twenty, it's a whole pod of whales.

THE TALL ONE: They're blowing out air.

THE BEAUTIFUL ONE: And they're moving so quickly. I thought they'd be slow but they're/

THE TALL ONE: /They're coming towards us. They want to eat us.

THE BURLY ONE: What? No. Whales eat plankton.

THE TALL ONE: But they're headed right for us.

THE BEAUTIFUL ONE: There's so many of them.

THE BURLY ONE: Why are there so many whales, all together, moving so quickly? Where the fuck are they going?

We hear THE STOCKY ONE's voice.

THE STOCKY ONE: The term "whale" denotes, in the broadest sense, any large sized cetacean: sperm whales, fin whales, humpback whales and others.

THE BURLY ONE: Who's that?

THE STOCKY ONE: Whales are descendants of mammals which lived on dry land. Their ancestors began to adapt to aquatic life approximately 50 million years ago. Due to their habitat, whales are "conscious breathers": they decide when to breathe.

THE BURLY ONE: I read that on Wikipedia, that was me: whose voice is that?

THE STOCKY ONE: Whales sleep like all other mammals, with the sole difference that they cannot fall unconscious for long, precisely because they must remain conscious in order to

breathe. This problem is resolved by only one half of their
brain being asleep at any time.

*There is a loud noise, as if something has collided with the container. The
light flickers off and on again. The sound of rushing water.*

THE BURLY ONE: What's happening? What the fuck is going on?

THE STOCKY ONE: Eubaleana glacialis, more commonly known
as the "right whale", is a species of whale still found in
the North Atlantic, though currently at risk of extinction.
In early autumn, this large cetacean can often be found
feasting on zooplankton in the Bay of Fundy, between
Nova Scotia and New Brunswick. Canadian researchers
have been documenting this event since 1980, estimating
that it can often involve over a hundred whales, out of an
estimated total worldwide population of five hundred. This
year, however, only a dozen or so whales could be seen: the
lowest number recorded for thirty-four years. According to
monitoring work by the New England Aquarium, this sudden
drop in numbers should not necessarily be seen as a sign of
further decline in an already nearly extinct species: according
to many marine biologists, the missing Eubaleana glacialis
must just have gone elsewhere.

THE BEAUTIFUL ONE: This reduction in whale numbers in
historical areas of abundant food supply is occurring within
a context of great ecosystem change in the entire North East
Atlantic area. Researchers at the New England Aquarium
studying right whales do not attribute these migratory
changes to any singular factor, though climate change is
high on the list. It seems these right whales have sought out
alternate currents in order to reach alternate feeding areas.

THE TALL ONE: A fundamental component of the diet of
these cetaceans is the miniscule Calanus finmarchicus,
which researchers noted as being in decline in the Bay of
Fundy over the summer months of last year. Meanwhile, at
Cape Cod Bay, where whales can usually be found in large
numbers, other scientists have noted higher concentrations of
Calanus finmarchicus; so much so, in fact, that these usually

colourless creatures are starting to alter the colour of the bay's water. Furthermore, according to recent studies, water temperatures in areas such as the Gulf of Maine have been slowly increasing, causing various marine species, including the cod and the red hake, to move further north.

THE BEAUTIFUL ONE: Increased precipitation, and the rapid melting of ice caps in the Arctic, Greenland and Canada, and the increased sweet water currents this creates in the North West Atlantic, is causing increased stratification of ocean waters, and a change in the quantity and distribution of phytoplankton and zooplankton, at the base of the food chains of many species.

THE TALL ONE: But the gradual disappearance of Canadian right whales remains a mystery.

The light returns. THE BURLY ONE has disappeared. THE TALL ONE and THE BEAUTIFUL ONE hold hands.

THE STOCKY ONE: Migrations are movements that animals make periodically along well-defined routes, often over very large distances. But they are always followed by a return to the place of departure. They may be triggered by causes related to reproduction, such as the search for a suitable place for mating, nesting or raising offspring, or by periodical environmental difficulties, such as the arrival of a cold season in temperate regions.

Slow lights down.

END

ALSO AVAILABLE FROM SALAMANDER STREET

All Salamander Street plays can be bought in bulk at a discount for performance or study. Contact info@salamanderstreet.com to enquire about performance liscenses.

Group Portrait in a Summer Landscape
by Peter Arnott
Paperback ISBN: 9781914228933
eBook ISBN: 9781914228957

An intense and riveting play set in a Perthshire country house during the Scottish Independence referendum of 2014. A retired academic and political heavyweight invites family and former students together for a dramatic reckoning.

Chatsky and Miser, Miser! by Anthony Burgess
Paperback ISBN: 9781914228889
eBook ISBN: 9781914228308

Anthony Burgess expertly tackles the major monuments of French and Russian theatre: *The Miser* by Molière and *Chatsky* by Alexander Griboyedov. Burgess's recently discovered verse and prose plays are published for the first time in this volume.

Placeholder by Catherine Bisset
ISBN: 9781914228919
eBook ISBN: 9781914228940

Profoundly thought-provoking, this solo play about the historical actor-singer of colour known as 'Minette' offers an exploration of the complex racial and social dynamics of what would become the first independent nation in the Caribbean.

Outlier by Malaika Kegode
ISBN: 9781914228339

Genre-defying and emotional, *Outlier* explores the impact of isolation, addiction and friendship on young people.

www.ingramcontent.com/pod-product-compliance
Lightning Source LLC
Jackson TN
JSHW011942131224
75386JS00041B/1518